AN ADVENT JOURNEY

An Advent Journey

FOLLOWING THE SEED FROM EDEN TO BETHLEHEM

JEFF ANDERSON

TABLE OF CONTENTS

WELCOME TO THE JOURNEY!

When reading the Bible we often skip the genealogies. The names are long and hard to pronounce. But what if we saw the lineage of Jesus as an epic tale of survival, battle, and victory?

For a period of roughly 4,000 years, the Seed of Adam leads to an expectant mother and father in a town called Bethlehem.

Read with us this Advent Season, for 25 days, and we'll explore how 64 generations (64 families) prepare for the arrival of Jesus.

You'll see how some of the Bible's most famous stories – and some unfamiliar ones – are connected to the Christ child.

The Seed helps us make sense of the story, and appreciate the flow of the Bible. The Seed helps us see the Old Testament minutia in a dramatic light. The Seed helps us appreciate the history of Christ.

For parents and adults, this 25-day series will help you see the big picture of the Bible together, in just five minutes per day—beginning December 1st.

Children can see that the manger in Bethlehem is not an isolated feel-good Bible story, but a promise that's been plainly in process since the Garden of Eden.

HOW TO USE

Each of the 25 days includes the following:

> ➤ New name(s) in the line of the Seed (64 names total)

> ➤ Genealogy text from scriptures

> ➤ Brief summary for the day's lesson

> ➤ "Afterthought" to go deeper in family discussions

You can experience each day's reading in 5 minutes or less. Or you can take 10-15 minutes to discuss themes more deeply with your family. Find the format and pace that best fits you and your family.

If you get off track, don't sweat it. It's easy to cover multiple days and catch up.

Also I love to hear about your family journey, insights and experiences. Please don't hesitate to email me at Jeff@JeffAndersonAuthor.com

DISCUSSING THE SEED WITH CHILDREN

Parents, introduce the Seed concept however appropriate for your family.

For my teenage sons, years ago I actually used the biblical theme of the Seed to talk about the "birds and bees." Discussions were made easier discussing God's design for sex and marriage – by discussing the transfer of the Seed.

For my eleven year old daughter, her knowledge of the Seed is much more basic. She understands babies come from a mommy and daddy seed, without needing to know much about sex.

If appropriate, let the Seed help you have these important conversations with your family.

APPENDICES

Be sure to note these resources at the back of this e-book.

Appendix A – Tracking the Seed, from Adam to Christ

Appendix B – Notes on Bible Genealogies

Appendix C – Bible Timeline Calculations (Day 6)

DAY 1

THE SEED

Introduction

[Scheduled Reading: Genesis 3:15]

And I will put enmity between you and the woman, and between your seed and her seed; he shall bruise you on the head, and you shall bruise him on the heel. (NASB)

If there was ever a verse that spelled B-O-O-M!, it just might be Genesis 3:15. It's loaded. Like the hammer effect when a courtroom judge drops the gavel on the table.

After Adam and Eve sinned, and before God cursed mankind and the earth, God cursed the serpent. He delivered a guilty verdict… and a forecast of what was to come.

There's going to be a **Seed**—Jesus—who will come from the family line of Adam and Eve. The serpent (Satan) will harass creation and strike the heel of Jesus. In the end, Jesus will "crush" Satan's head (using NIV language).

Genesis 3:15 is one of the most foundational verses in the Bible. In fact, it tells the story of the Bible.

From Genesis 3:15 forward, the rest of the Bible is all about working out this verse. Streaks of evil seek to threaten the Seed's survival. But God always responds, sometimes with a climactic event, keeping the Seed on course.

Eventually, sixty-plus generations after Adam, this Holy Spirit "Seed" arrives. Baby Jesus.

This is what Advent is all about - the ultimate arrival of The Seed in a town called Bethlehem nearly two thousand years ago.

After the miracle birth in Bethlehem, Jesus grows up, walks the earth, dies a crucifixion death and miraculously rises again.

This resurrection event is a crushing blow to the serpent, but not the final blow. (Spoiler alert!) That comes in the book of Revelation.

Genesis 3:15 is a mind-numbing prophecy and sums up the Bible narrative in roughly 30 words.

Each day this Advent season, we'll track the fathers in line of the Seed.

We'll also look at the Bible's big-picture themes and marvel at how God's sovereignty, through His Seed strategy, set up this grand event we celebrate each Christmas Day... the birth of Jesus Christ.

Did you ever think: while in the Garden of Eden,
God had already planned the arrival of Jesus in Bethlehem?

DAY 2

THE RACE IS ON

Adam (1) & Seth (2)

[Scheduled Reading: Genesis 5:1-8]

*¹This is the book of the generations of **Adam**. When God created man, he made him in the likeness of God. ²Male and female he created them, and he blessed them and named them Man when they were created. ³When Adam had lived 130 years, he fathered a son in his own likeness, after his image, and named him Seth.⁴The days of Adam after he fathered **Seth** were 800 years; and he had other sons and daughters. ⁵Thus all the days that Adam lived were 930 years, and he died.*

⁶When Seth had lived 105 years, he fathered Enosh. ⁷Seth lived after he fathered Enosh 807 years and had other sons and daughters. ⁸Thus all the days of Seth were 912 years, and he died.

The Bible genealogy starts with a man named **Adam**. He is known as the 1ˢᵗ Adam. He named his wife Eve, meaning "mother of all the living."

Adam is referred to as the "son of God," (Luke 3:38) meaning that he was created directly by God (from the dust of the ground). He was not born from the seed of an earthly father.

When Adam and Eve sinned, death entered the scene. The curse of death was not only for humans but also for animals… grass… trees… etc. Nothing would live forever.

Death was initially a slow process and explains why man lived for hundreds of years.

God knew this death pattern was not sustainable. That's the reason for His Seed plan.

From Genesis 3:15, the countdown begins toward a 2nd Adam. Think of this as a "do-over" Adam. A remake. A second attempt to establish God's perfect creation.

This 2nd Adam would be a perfect, sinless man that would one day redeem man's fallen condition.

God could have redeemed Adam immediately. With the snap of the fingers, Adam #2 could have entered the garden.

Or God could have introduced this redeemer seed in a second generation… or in three generations. Or maybe ten.

But God chose sixty plus generations of fathers – over approximately 4,000 years - to arrive at this 2nd Adam.

Adam and Eve had two sons, Cain and Abel. What beautiful creature boys they must have been. Perhaps one of them could transfer the Seed forward.

But Satan was at work. Tragedy stuck again. Cain killed Abel. Not a good start for the Seed journey.

So Eve bore another son to Adam and named him **Seth**. God chose to route the Seed through Seth. Why did God route the Seed through Seth and not Cain or some other son?

We don't know. We'll learn that's the case with all God's decisions regarding the line of the Seed.

God's sovereignty prevails.

Sometimes the line of the Seed makes sense from our perspective. Other times it doesn't.

But from Adam to Seth, the first transfer of the Seed is in the books.

And for our Advent Journey, following the Seed to Bethlehem… the race is on!

When we think of Eve, we mostly think of her sin in the garden. But consider Eve as a mother of children.

How devastating must it have been for Eve to lose a child to the violence of a sibling?

Do you think Eve had any idea how the "seed of the woman" (Gen. 3:15) would one day redeem man's fallen nature?

DAY 3
ADAM & EVE... & FRED FLINTSTONE

Enos/Enosh (3) & Cainan/Kenan (4)

[Scheduled Reading: Genesis 5:9-14]

*⁹ When **Enosh** had lived 90 years, he fathered **Kenan**. ¹⁰ Enosh lived after he fathered Kenan 815 years and had other sons and daughters. ¹¹ Thus all the days of Enosh were 905 years, and he died. ¹² When Kenan had lived 70 years, he fathered Mahalalel. ¹³ Kenan lived after he fathered Mahalalel 840 years and had other sons and daughters. ¹⁴ Thus all the days of Kenan were 910 years, and he died.*

There's growing debate about the historical placement of Adam. How long ago was he on earth? Based on the Bible's genealogical accounts, we can date the account of Adam to roughly 4,000 BC.

Yet even Christians still have questions: *Was Adam even real? Perhaps Adam and Eve were figurative characters? Is Genesis completely true? Maybe it's poetic!*

Here's the problem. If Adam was not real, then when did Bible characters become real people? At what point did Bible cartoons become Bible history?

If we can't trust the accounts of Adam, then what about Noah? Or Abraham? Or David?

Is the Bible part history and part make-believe?

For our Advent journey, we're taking time to get to know each generation in the line of Christ. Because the Bible contains careful genealogical accounts, we're treating them seriously.

After Adam and Seth, we arrive at **Enos** and then **Cainan** (Enosh and Kenan are the Hebrew names).

We know very little about these men. But the Bible tells us their placement in the line of the Seed – their age when they had sons and their age when they died.

In a sense, the Bible is a of collection birth certificates. It's an official book of names and families – these families are connected by God's sovereignty to bring about the Seed.

Each of these fathers have a place in biblical history. Some of these names are familiar to us as the Bible contains a fuller account of their lives.

Other names - like Enos and Cainan - are unfamiliar. All we know is where they fit in the line of the Seed.

For me, these men are as real as men like Abraham Lincoln or Benjamin Franklin. I've never met Lincoln or Franklin, but I believe they truly existed in our history.

I don't personally know the fathers in the path of the Seed (Enos, Cainan, etc), but I believe in their role in the Advent Journey.

Does it surprise you that Christians who claim to believe the Bible still question the existence of characters in the Bible's genealogies? What would you tell them?

Bible Reading Tip!

Kenan and Enos are Hebrew names (Old Testament). Cainan and Enosh are Greek names (New Testament). Depending on your Bible translation, sometimes a name variation can be a completely different name, but most often a name variation will be minor.

For this Advent Journey, I've used mostly names and scripture references from the ESV Bible translation.

11

DAY 4

FAITH LEGACY

Mahalalel (5), Jared (6), Enoch (7), Methuselah (8) & Lamech (9)

[Scheduled Reading: Genesis 5:12-31]

¹² When Kenan had lived 70 years, he fathered **Mahalalel***. ¹³ Kenan lived after he fathered Mahalalel 840 years and had other sons and daughters. ¹⁴ Thus all the days of Kenan were 910 years, and he died.*

¹⁵ When Mahalalel had lived 65 years, he fathered **Jared***. ¹⁶ Mahalalel lived after he fathered Jared 830 years and had other sons and daughters. ¹⁷ Thus all the days of Mahalalel were 895 years, and he died.*

¹⁸ When Jared had lived 162 years, he fathered **Enoch***. ¹⁹ Jared lived after he fathered Enoch 800 years and had other sons and daughters. ²⁰ Thus all the days of Jared were 962 years, and he died.*

²¹ When Enoch had lived 65 years, he fathered **Methuselah***. ²² Enoch walked with God after he fathered Methuselah 300 years and had other sons and daughters. ²³ Thus all the days of Enoch were 365 years. ²⁴ Enoch walked with God, and he was not, for God took him.*

²⁵ When Methuselah had lived 187 years, he fathered **Lamech***. ²⁶ Methuselah lived after he fathered Lamech 782 years and had other sons and daughters. ²⁷ Thus all the days of Methuselah were 969 years, and he died.*

²⁸ When Lamech had lived 182 years, he fathered a son ²⁹ and called his name Noah, saying, "Out of the ground that the Lord has cursed, this one shall bring us relief from our work and from the painful toil of our hands." ³⁰ Lamech lived after he fathered Noah 595 years and had other sons and daughters. ³¹ Thus all the days of Lamech were 777 years, and he died.

After Adam, Seth, Enos and Cainan (Days 2 & 3) – we have **Mahalaleel and Jared.** We know very little of these two fathers. Next we arrive at **Enoch**.

Enoch was special. He's one of only two men who never died (the other is Elijah). One day he was on earth, then one day "he was not; for God took him" (Genesis 5:24).

The Bible says he "walked with God." What an impressive three-word resumé! His God-pleasing reputation places him among the Bible's "Faith Hall of Fame" members (see Hebrews 11:5).

And if you flip all the way to the end of your Bible to a book called Jude, Enoch is mentioned as "the seventh from Adam" (v14,15).

For all of us seed trackers, what number is Enoch in the line of the Seed? That's right. #7!

That's proof that Bible authors like Jude relied on the Genesis genealogies, too.

Next we have **Methuselah.** He's the oldest living man mentioned in the Bible. He lived to be 969 years old.

Methuselah held a stunning position in faith history. His father (Enoch) was a spiritual giant.

On the other side of history, Methuselah was Noah's grandfather!

Based on Bible records, Methuselah died in the year of the flood. He watched the ark project start with blueprints and likely saw its completion. He might have swung hammers with Noah and sons (Methuselah's great grandsons).

It's hard for us to fathom how these men could have lived to be 800 or 900 years old. But remember, man was created to live forever. And the death process set in slowly.

Methuselah's son, **Lamech** must have caught his father and grandfather's faith, and he must have sensed God's redemptive plan at work.

When his son, Noah, was born, Lamech prophesied saying, "This one shall bring us relief..." (Gen. 5:29).

What is this "relief", or "comfort" as other translations say, Lamech is talking about?

We're about to find out.

> *Think about the amazing spiritual legacy of Enoch, Methuselah, Lamech and Noah.*
>
> *What does the spiritual legacy look like for your family - do you come from a line of Christ followers? Or did you come to faith in other ways besides your family?*
>
> *Whatever your family's faith story, take time to thank God for bringing you into faith and salvation.*

DAY 5

RELIEF FOR THE SEED

Noah (10)

[Scheduled Reading: Genesis 5:28-32]

²⁸ *When Lamech had lived 182 years, he fathered a son* ²⁹ *and called his name* **Noah**, *saying, "Out of the ground that the Lord has cursed,* **this one shall bring us relief from our work and from the painful toil of our hands."* ³⁰ *Lamech lived after he fathered Noah 595 years and had other sons and daughters.* ³¹ *Thus all the days of Lamech were 777 years, and he died.* ³² *After Noah was 500 years old, Noah fathered Shem, Ham, and Japheth.*

Let's review the big picture.

A battle was being waged between good and evil… between God and Satan.

After God created man, Satan tempted man with sin. Because of sin, death was introduced to the world.

But the repetitive cycle of life and death was not a good long-term plan. God's solution was a special Seed to break the death cycle (remember Genesis 3:15).

This seed was a 2ⁿᵈ Adam. A sinless Adam. Jesus.

God took His time working out this plan. It had been just over one thousand years from Adam's placement in the garden to Noah's birth.

Meanwhile wickedness was reaching intolerable levels. Enoch likely sensed it. Methuselah and Lamech sensed it as well.

How intolerable? The Bible says God regretted that He made man on earth. He was grieved in his heart. (It's hard to fathom these emotions from God - see Genesis 6:6).

God was ready to wipe the earth clear of all life (6:7).

But what about the Seed? Would God abandon His plan from Genesis 3:15?

Never! God's covenants always stand.

God sent a global flood to destroy life on earth, but He spared one family. His start-over plan consisted of Noah and his wife, his three sons, and their wives. Eight people.

The Seed journey will continue.

After the flood, Noah un-boarded the ark and offered sacrifices of some of the clean animals to God.

Something about this blood-shedding event pleased God. So God put a rainbow in the sky and covenanted to never destroy the earth with water again.

But something deeper was going on in God's mind – something Noah could not see.

Noah's sacrifice was a foreshadowing of a future sacrifice God had planned for us.

Jesus, the eventual Seed, would one day offer himself as a living sacrifice, as final atonement for the sins of the world.

Lamech (Noah's father) was right. God did have something special planned for Noah (the one who "shall bring us relief.")

God used Noah to keep the Seed alive... and on track for the journey to Bethlehem.

Instead of an ark to save Noah's family, God could have destroyed everyone (including Noah) and started over with a new garden and a new Adam... or something different.

How does the Genesis 3:15 promise impact God's decision to continue with the seed of Adam?

DAY 6

LEAD ACTOR

Shem (11), Arphaxad (12), Salah (13), Eber (14), Peleg (15), Reu (16), Serug (17), Nahor (18)

[Scheduled Reading: Genesis 11:10-24]

*¹⁰These are the generations of **Shem**. When Shem was 100 years old, he fathered **Arpachshad** two years after the flood. ¹¹And Shem lived after he fathered Arpachshad 500 years and had other sons and daughters.*

*¹²When Arpachshad had lived 35 years, he fathered **Shelah**. ¹³And Arpachshad lived after he fathered Shelah 403 years and had other sons and daughters.*

*¹⁴When Shelah had lived 30 years, he fathered **Eber**. ¹⁵And Shelah lived after he fathered Eber 403 years and had other sons and daughters.*

*¹⁶When Eber had lived 34 years, he fathered **Peleg**. ¹⁷And Eber lived after he fathered Peleg 430 years and had other sons and daughters.*

*¹⁸When Peleg had lived 30 years, he fathered **Reu**. ¹⁹And Peleg lived after he fathered Reu 209 years and had other sons and daughters.*

*²⁰When Reu had lived 32 years, he fathered **Serug**. ²¹And Reu lived after he fathered Serug 207 years and had other sons and daughters.*

*²²When Serug had lived 30 years, he fathered **Nahor**. ²³And Serug lived after he fathered Nahor 200 years and had other sons and daughters.*

²⁴When Nahor had lived 29 years, he fathered Terah. ²⁵And Nahor lived after he fathered Terah 119 years and had other sons and daughters.

Genesis 5 provides the careful genealogy from Adam to Noah – the first ten generations. Genesis 11 traces the Seed for the next ten generations.

If you glance at Genesis Chapter 10, you'll notice the genealogies for each of Noah's three sons – Shem, Ham and Japheth. But Chapter 11 circles back around to offer ages and life spans for just Shem's descendants.

Why does scripture provide greater detail for just Shem's line? *Answer: Because that's the line of the Seed.*

From Noah, God routed the Seed (from Adam to Jesus) through the line of **Shem**. And the Bible provides greater detail for Shem's line since the Seed is the Bible's featured family.

Just as the star character in a play gets special attention, the line of the Seed gets the "headliner" treatment all throughout scriptures. We'll see this clearly throughout this Advent Journey.

Very little is known about the six fathers after Shem leading up to **Nahor**, except for their ages when their sons were born and the years they lived thereafter.

God gives us this detail so we can piece together a working chronology.

It's a mostly silent era in scriptures. But things are about to get very interesting for this Advent Journey.

From Adam to Abraham is roughly 2,000 years. With the help of Genesis 5 & 11, and a calculator, we can calculate certain time periods. Go ahead – try it with your family!

a. How many years is it from Adam to Noah's flood?

b. How many years from the flood to Abraham?

See Appendix C for calculations

[Answers: a. 1,656 years, b. 292 years]

DAY 7

LEAVING SIN CITY

Terah (19)

[Scheduled Reading: Genesis 11:27-32]

*²⁷Now these are the generations of **Terah**. Terah fathered Abram, Nahor, and Haran; and Haran fathered Lot. ²⁸Haran died in the presence of his father Terah in the land of his kindred, in Ur of the Chaldeans. ²⁹And Abram and Nahor took wives. The name of Abram's wife was Sarai, and the name of Nahor's wife, Milcah, the daughter of Haran the father of Milcah and Iscah. ³⁰Now Sarai was barren; she had no child.*

³¹Terah took Abram his son and Lot the son of Haran, his grandson, and Sarai his daughter-in-law, his son Abram's wife, and they went forth together from Ur of the Chaldeans to go into the land of Canaan, but when they came to Haran, they settled there. ³² The days of Terah were 205 years, and Terah died in Haran.

Terah receives very little mention in scripture. But his role in Biblical history was monumental.

Terah was responsible for getting Abram (tomorrow's Seed guest) away from "sin city."

Terah's clan was from a place called Ur, a neighboring city to Babylon located in the Mesopotamian region.

If you look at a historical map, it was quite a journey from Ur to Haran where Terah and his family initially settled. From there God called Abram (Genesis 12) to distance himself further away to the land of Canaan (which includes present day Israel).

So what's behind this cross-country move?

God was accomplishing separation for Abram and his family. Babylon and nearby cities (i.e. Ur) were a highly cultural and political mecca with flourishing arts and commerce and ideas… and rampant worship of a host of gods.

Centuries earlier Babylon suffered God's judgment for its "Tower of Babel" experiment. God dispersed its inhabitants across the earth to slow down their progressive ways of thinking (i.e. a tower toward the heavens).

Just like progressive cultures today, being on the cutting edge of culture often means being on the cutting edge of sin.

Throughout scriptures, Babylon is the symbol for just about everything that Eden initially was not - SIN.

Whenever God calls out evil and gives it a figurative reference, He frequently mentions "Babylon."

In the book of Revelation, an angel from heaven describes "Babylon the Great" as a "dwelling place for demons" (18:2).

Another reason for getting away from Ur was the practicality of space. God was preparing to birth a new nation. Fresh land was needed to support the growing nation of fathers in the line of the Seed.

Getting Abram out of Ur (and away from Babylon) and situated in a new land was very purposeful.

For the next two thousand years, Biblical history would be focused primarily on the land of Canaan and, at times, nearby Egypt.

And what little town was located in the heart of Canaan? Yes, Bethlehem!

Look online at a map of ancient Babylon. Locate the nearby city of Ur. And if you Google the location of the "Garden of Eden," where was it likely located?

Not far from Babylon!

Can you see why God was interested in relocating Terah's family to a new land?

DAY 8

SPECIAL FATHER

Abraham, formerly Abram (20)

[Scheduled Reading: Genesis 12:1-9]

*¹Now the Lord said to **Abram**, "Go from your country and your kindred and your father's house to the land that I will show you. ²And I will make of you a great nation, and I will bless you and make your name great, so that you will be a blessing. ³I will bless those who bless you, and him who dishonors you I will curse, and in you all the families of the earth shall be blessed."*

⁴So Abram went, as the Lord had told him, and Lot went with him. Abram was seventy-five years old when he departed from Haran. ⁵And Abram took Sarai his wife, and Lot his brother's son, and all their possessions that they had gathered, and the people that they had acquired in Haran, and they set out to go to the land of Canaan. When they came to the land of Canaan, ⁶Abram passed through the land to the place at Shechem, to the oak of Moreh. At that time the Canaanites were in the land. ⁷Then the Lord appeared to Abram and said, "To your offspring I will give this land." So he built there an altar to the Lord, who had appeared to him. ⁸From there he moved to the hill country on the east of Bethel and pitched his tent, with Bethel on the west and Ai on the east. And there he built an altar to the Lord and called upon the name of the Lord. ⁹And Abram journeyed on, still going toward the Negeb.

The path to Bethlehem included some legendary characters... special men and women used by God to route the Seed through strategic pivot points.

26

Aside from Christ Jesus of course, Abraham (formerly Abram) might arguably be the most legendary character of the entire line of the Seed.

History's most notable, lasting movements are led by special father figures. An example on a much smaller scale would be George Washington. A person of unique pedigree. A true father to a lasting movement.

It's hard to put in words what Abraham meant for Israel. Very few men had the personal favor and attention from God quite like Abraham – visits from angels, conversations with God, gigantic favor and gigantic tests, etc.

The single word that sums up Abraham is "Father." (I'm really trying to not be influenced by the "Father Abraham" song from Sunday school).

He's the father to the Jews. He's father to the Christians. Oddly, he's also father to Islam (long story involving a son named Ishmael).

Most importantly, He's Father to The Seed – Jesus.

Abraham was not only a special father. He was a faith giant, a distinguished military leader... and a wealthy businessman. Like Billy Graham, George Washington and John Rockefeller all in one.

God's strategy was to launch a new people group that would form a new identity for the Seed. God desired a new family to pivot the Seed away from Babylon and toward this new chosen land.

Launching this new family-nation required just the right person. A man of impeccable faith, a determined leader, an astute fighter, and a balance sheet to garner the respect of foreign kings he encountered along the way.

To prepare Abraham for this fatherhood privilege, God had some monumental tests for him.

Test of belief. God promised to give Abraham and his wife Sarah (formerly Sarai) a son (Isaac) in their very old age. The promise included countless ancestors. From God's perspective, this "seed" would one day lead to Jesus.

Abraham has no idea how significant his seed would be. Overall they passed this test, although initially they weren't sure and tried to help God by having a son (Ishmael) through a maidservant (Hagar).

This weak moment would have long-lasting implications, giving Satan a foothold to introduce a false religion (Islam) that still thrives to this day.

Test of obedience. When Isaac grew to be a young lad, God asked Abraham to sacrifice him (yes, to kill his own son!). It's an unthinkable request today and it was then, too.

Abraham passed the obedience test (more on that tomorrow).

Passing these great tests came with great responsibilities. Sure enough, God affirmed His previous promise, to make Abraham father to many nations and to give God's chosen nation a special land.

This land was not the crowded, sin-polluted land near Babylon – but a special land called Canaan that would one day house a little town called... Bethlehem.

Big assignments from God often follow big tests. What test(s) has God had for you, and how has that season of testing prepared you for something special?

In Genesis, there's very little mention about Terah's son, Nahor (Abraham's brother). Why is there so much Bible attention to Abraham and nothing about Nahor?

Answer: Because Abraham is in the line of the Seed

Once again, the Bible is largely focused on families that fall in the line of the Seed.

DAY 9

FORESHADOW

Isaac (21)

[Scheduled Reading: Genesis 21:1-7]

¹ The Lord visited Sarah as he had said, and the Lord did to Sarah as he had promised. ² And Sarah conceived and bore Abraham a son in his old age at the time of which God had spoken to him. ³ Abraham called the name of his son who was born to him, whom Sarah bore him, **Isaac.** *⁴ And Abraham circumcised his son Isaac when he was eight days old, as God had commanded him. ⁵ Abraham was a hundred years old when his son Isaac was born to him. ⁶ And Sarah said, "God has made laughter for me; everyone who hears will laugh over me." ⁷ And she said, "Who would have said to Abraham that Sarah would nurse children? Yet I have borne him a son in his old age."*

We're about to shift gears in our Seed journey.

Genesis Chapters 1-11 race through the first twenty generations – from Adam to Noah, and then Shem to Abraham.

For the remainder of Genesis – 39 chapters – the biblical story slows to a crawl, covering just four generations.

The accounts of Abraham, Isaac and Jacob (the Bible's famous patriarchs) and Jacob's sons - are crucial to piecing together the biblical narrative.

Today we look at the legacy of Isaac.

The parallels between Isaac and Jesus are stunning. Both arrived by divine birth.

Isaac was born to Abraham and Sarah in their very old age. Jesus was born to Mary, an unwed mother impregnated by a Seed from heaven (conceived by the Holy Spirit).

Another parallel is a famous self-sacrifice. (Genesis 22)

When God asked Abraham to sacrifice his son Isaac, it was an unthinkable request. Would God really require such a thing?

Abraham was committed to obedience. Isaac (somewhere between being an adolescent boy and a young man) was old enough to be a willing participant as he carried the wood on his shoulders to the place of worship.

This story is one we struggle to fully appreciate. It's far outside the realm of anything that's ever been requested by God. In fact, it just might be the most ridiculous request ever.

Scriptures are full of seemingly bizarre instructions from God.

March around a city for seven days blowing trumpets (Joshua). Have men drink water from a brook as a way to select an army (Gideon). Marry a prostitute who continues to be unfaithful, have children with her and give them ridiculous, embarrassing names (prophet Hosea, named his daughters "No Mercy" and "Not My People").

But nothing fits the category of "sacrifice your only son." Especially if the son was a miracle child born in your old age – and the son through whom God promised to birth a great nation!

But Abraham and Isaac cooperated. God stopped Abraham short of sacrificing Isaac and provided a ram for the blood sacrifice instead.

So what did God possibly have in mind for this sacrifice request?

Probably a scene that would unfold 2,000 years later on a nearby mountain. Jesus would carry his wood (a wooden cross) up a hill for his own sacrifice.

Unlike with Abraham and Isaac, God did go through with the crucifixion death of His Son (even Jesus asked for a way out).

31

The near sacrifice of Isaac was a foreshadowing – a picture - of a future sacrifice (Jesus on the cross).

God knew He would one day sacrifice His Son, just as He had asked Abraham to do.

As for Isaac, he took on the role of Jesus – the object of a sacrifice. With an audience in heaven, Isaac rehearsed the sacrifice that would come two thousand years later.

Isaac demonstrated obedience and submission to the same act that would one day become the most selfless act known to man.

How impressive was Isaac's almost-sacrifice? You could even say Jesus had an advantage that Isaac did not. Jesus knew the outcome and purpose of his death on the cross. Isaac was not so sure. He was clueless. He was simply trusting God…with his life.

How fitting that God would route the path of the Seed through a man (Abraham) and his son (Isaac) – two men who would demonstrate unusual faith to carry out a similar sacrifice that God and Jesus would one day perform.

Stunning story. Stunning symbolism. Stunning faith.

A child sacrifice does not make sense to us and we can be sure God would never ask that of us today. But what is an example of something God might ask us to sacrifice – or maybe a sacrifice we have made - in order to step into His larger plan for our lives?

(Discuss as a family. This could be a personal or family sacrifice – i.e. giving up a job or promotion, a family relocation, a financial gift, a call to ministry, etc.)

DAY 10

12 SONS, 12 TRIBES

Jacob (22)

[Scheduled Reading: Genesis 25:19-28; Genesis 35:22-26]

[19] *These are the generations of Isaac, Abraham's son: Abraham fathered Isaac,* [20] *and Isaac was forty years old when he took Rebekah, the daughter of Bethuel the Aramean of Paddan-aram, the sister of Laban the Aramean, to be his wife.* [21] *And Isaac prayed to the Lord for his wife, because she was barren. And the Lord granted his prayer, and Rebekah his wife conceived.* [22] *The children struggled together within her, and she said, "If it is thus, why is this happening to me?"[1] So she went to inquire of the Lord.* [23] *And the Lord said to her,*

"Two nations are in your womb, and two peoples from within you shall be divided; the one shall be stronger than the other, the older shall serve the younger."

[24] *When her days to give birth were completed, behold, there were twins in her womb.* [25] *The first came out red, all his body like a hairy cloak, so they called his name Esau.* [26] *Afterward his brother came out with his hand holding Esau's heel, so his name was called* **Jacob.** *Isaac was sixty years old when she bore them.*

[27] *When the boys grew up, Esau was a skillful hunter, a man of the field, while Jacob was a quiet man, dwelling in tents.* [28] *Isaac loved Esau because he ate of his game, but Rebekah loved Jacob.*

Genesis 35:

Now the sons of Jacob were twelve. [23] *The sons of Leah: Reuben (Jacob's firstborn), Simeon, Levi, Judah, Issachar, and Zebulun.* [24] *The sons of Rachel: Joseph and Benjamin.* [25] *The sons of Bilhah, Rachel's servant: Dan and Naphtali.* [26] *The sons of*

Zilpah, Leah's servant: Gad and Asher. These were the sons of Jacob who were born to him in Paddan-aram.

Jacob lived a high-drama life. He grew up competing with his twin brother, Esau (eventually stealing his birthright).

He worked seven years for a wife he didn't choose – then another seven years for the wife he did choose.

He wrestled with an angel of God.

He received a famous name change (from Jacob to "Israel").

His sons wreaked havoc on his family. They kidnapped their younger brother (the favored son, Joseph), sold him off to slavery and fabricated a story about a deadly animal attack.

(Does this count as a dysfunctional family?)

Still, Jacob's most significant life contribution might just be his twelve problematic sons. These twelve sons resulted in twelve mighty tribes.

These tribes would become God's strategy for organizing and protecting the new nation of "Israel," (the Israelites).

And protecting Israel meant protecting the Seed!

Back to the big picture. While Satan was working feverishly to destroy the Seed, God was building them for survival.

Like any thriving nation, this Israelite nation would one day need to be strong, independent, well financed, heavily armed. They would need government that could sustain order.

God accomplished these functions through the twelve-tribe alliance. The member tribes worked together to share land, share a unified army, share governance, share in the welfare of the poor and widows, etc.

Much like the thirteen colonies that governed the new America, these twelve tribes governed the new nation called Israel.

But only one of the tribes could transfer the Seed? Which tribe would have that special honor?

Using our own system of government today, discuss the various ways God organized the twelve tribes.

- For a congress, they had Levites.

- For a president, they had a prophet (initially Moses).

- Instead of member states, they had member tribes.

- Instead of a democracy (governed by the people), they were a theocracy — (ruled by God).

- God gave them laws and regulations (see Leviticus, Numbers, Deuteronomy)

DAY 11

NOT WHAT YOU THINK

Judah (23)

[Scheduled Reading: Genesis 49:8-10]

*"**Judah**, your brothers shall praise you; your hand shall be on the neck of your enemies; your father's sons shall bow down before you. [9] Judah is a lion's cub; from the prey, my son, you have gone up. He stooped down; he crouched as a lion and as a lioness; who dares rouse him? [10] The scepter shall not depart from Judah, nor the ruler's staff from between his feet, until tribute comes to him; and to him shall be the obedience of the peoples.*

One thing we learn about the path of the Seed: God does not always choose the logical path — at least not from our perspective.

If I were to choose the path of the Seed from the twelve sons of Jacob, I would choose Joseph - a man of impeccable character, with an impressive faith and work resumé.

He saved his family from a famine – even after they kidnapped and sold him years earlier.

But God didn't route the Seed through Joseph. God chose Judah, one of the older brothers (yeah, one of the kidnappers!)

Years after the kidnapping, Joseph rose to power in Egypt (fascinating story covering Genesis chapters 37, 39-47).

During a dreadful famine in Canaan, Jacob sent his dysfunctional sons to Egypt to buy food. Their shocking encounter with Joseph set up an eventual family reunion – the brothers returned home to get Jacob and went back to live with Joseph in Egypt.

This detour to Egypt is a monumental pivot for the Seed – a survival measure orchestrated by God to keep the Seed alive.

Just before Jacob died he delivered a blessing to each of his twelve sons.

Judah's blessing reveals God's chosen path for the Seed.

The scepter shall not depart from Judah, nor the ruler's staff from between his feet, until tribute comes to him (Genesis 49:10).

The tribe of Judah would be represented by a line of kings...an eventual king who's reign will never end – King Jesus!

Jesus came from the Tribe of Judah. Judah's legacy echoes into the future.

Judah's actual life story was quite an embarrassment to the family tree. His legacy was not defined by honor or faith or leadership or military exploits.

Instead Judah was known for one of the Bible's classic family scandals (you'll see tomorrow).

And the Advent Journey continues ...

As a child growing up in church, I remember singing songs about "Father Abraham" and the "tribe of Judah." I had no idea the significance of these men as direct ancestors to Jesus.

How does tracking the Seed through the patriarchs help you to better appreciate the ancestry of Christ?

DAY 12

SCANDAL

Perez (24)

[Scheduled Reading: 1 Chronicles 2:1-4]

*These are the sons of Israel: Reuben, Simeon, Levi, Judah, Issachar, Zebulun, ² Dan, Joseph, Benjamin, Naphtali, Gad, and Asher. ³ The sons of Judah: Er, Onan and Shelah; these three Bath-shua the Canaanite bore to him. Now Er, Judah's firstborn, was evil in the sight of the Lord, and he put him to death. ⁴ His daughter-in-law Tamar also bore him **Perez** and Zerah. Judah had five sons in all.*

There are some strange stories in the Bible.

As you read certain accounts you might even wonder, "Why is this story here?"

Often, it's simply because of God's pattern of tracking the Seed—the family tree from Adam to Christ.

Jesus came from Abraham, Isaac, Jacob, Judah... then baby Perez, the child of Tamar.

And who exactly was this mother, Tamar? Well, it's quite a story! (Read Genesis 38).

Perez was conceived when his father, Judah, visited a pretending prostitute, who unbeknownst to him was his daughter-in-law, Tamar!

The short story is this: Judah's first two sons were killed by God because of their wickedness (not a very impressive parenting legacy).

According to tradition, Judah was expected to commit his third son to the widow of his deceased sons. (Tamar was the widow to the first son, and then the second son.) In this way, the Israelites fulfilled the duty of keeping the family name alive.

But Judah and Son #3 (Shelah) did not cooperate. So in God's divine and seemingly odd ways, He arranged for Judah an encounter with a lady disguised as a prostitute – who turned out to be his daughter-in-law, Tamar!

I know. Surprise!

Through Judah, Tamar had twin boys. The oldest, and the one in the line of the Seed, was baby Perez.

Stories like these show God's amazing sovereignty… and His desire to reveal for us the genealogy of Jesus Christ.

My maternal grandparents had no sons, only two daughters. So Grandpa's family name ceased to continue through him.

This is not a big deal today. But think about the significance of what this would mean for the line of the Seed!

Look at your own family tree. Can you identify examples where the family name ceased to continue?

DAY 13

SEED ESCORTS

Hezron (25), Ram (26) , Amminadab (27) , Nahshon (28)

[Scheduled Reading: 1 Chronicles 2:5-10; Ruth 4:18-20]

*⁵The sons of Perez: **Hezron** and Hamul. ⁶The sons of Zerah: Zimri, Ethan, Heman, Calcol, and Dara, five in all. ⁷The son of Carmi: Achan, the troubler of Israel, who broke faith in the matter of the devoted thing; ⁸and Ethan's son was Azariah.*

*⁹The sons of Hezron that were born to him: Jerahmeel, **Ram**, and Chelubai. ¹⁰Ram fathered **Amminadab**, and Amminadab fathered **Nahshon**, prince of the sons of Judah. (1 Chronicles 2:5-10).*

¹⁸Now these are the generations of Perez: Perez fathered Hezron, ¹⁹Hezron fathered Ram, Ram fathered Amminadab, ²⁰Amminadab fathered Nahshon, Nahshon fathered Salmon, (Ruth 4).

After Jacob's sons died, the families remained in Egypt (remember, they moved there to escape famine and live with Joseph). The Israelites multiplied quickly and eventually became slaves of the Egyptians.

Bible historians believe it was precisely 215 years from when Jacob's household relocated to Egypt with Joseph – to the time the Israelites were delivered from Egyptian slavery by a man named Moses (more on this man below).

Hezron (son of Perez) was among the seventy people of the "house of Jacob" (Gen. 46:12, 26, 27) who traveled to Egypt to live with Joseph.

42

During this 215 year period in Egypt, **Ram, Amminadab** and **Nahshon** were born.

Nahshon was the assigned military commander of the tribe of Judah, assembled under the leadership of Moses (Num. 1:7, 2:3, 10:14).

Nahshon had command of a force of 74,600 men. That's impressive authority! (Num. 1:26, 2:4).

While wandering in the wilderness, the Israelite leaders rebelled against God and spread negative reports throughout the twelve tribes. So God extended their wilderness vacation to forty years and did not let that generation enter the Promised Land (that's Canaan).

Nahshon's son, Salmon, was likely among the "little ones" (Num. 14:31) who grew up and crossed into the Promised Land with Joshua and Caleb.

And what's so famous about Salmon (besides his fishy name)? We'll save that for tomorrow.

Up until Abraham, the Bible has been mostly focused on characters in line of the Seed.

Joseph was the first major Bible character who fell outside the path of the Seed.

There's another faith champion who walked alongside the tribe of Judah to escort the Seed carriers – Moses, a Levite (tribe of Levi).

The next great leader outside the Seed line was Joshua (tribe of Ephraim). He succeeded Moses and had the awesome privilege of escorting the twelve tribes into the Promised Land.

Although men like Joseph, Moses and Joshua didn't fall directly in the line of the Seed, their role in the biblical story is critical.

Think of them as police escorts leading a VIP limo through a city. But instead of riding motorcycles with flashing lights, these men were fearless faith warriors, leading tens and hundreds of thousands of Israelites into battle to inhabit a very special land.

A land that would one day occupy a city…that occupies a manger…that houses an ordinary traveler and his pregnant wife who would give birth to this very special Seed.

We're getting closer to Bethlehem.

The twelve sons of Jacobs were brothers. All their children became cousins. And their children became second and third cousins… and their children became fourth and fifth cousins… and so on.

All of these Israelite characters were related: cousins to varying degrees.

To illustrate to your children how tribes (families) multiply over time, consider your own family and identify the lines of cousins (first, second, etc.) that they know (and don't know). Maybe you've had a family reunion in the past that can put this into context.

DAY 14

FAMOUS MOMS

Salmon (29), Boaz (30), Obed (31), Jesse (32)

[Scheduled Reading: 1 Chronicles 2:11-12; Ruth 4:21-22]

*Nahshon fathered **Salmon**, Salmon fathered **Boaz**, [12] Boaz fathered **Obed**, Obed fathered **Jesse**. (1 Chronicles 2:11-12).*

Salmon fathered Boaz, Boaz fathered Obed, [22] Obed fathered Jesse, and Jesse fathered David. *(Ruth 4:21-22).*

Bible Trivia Question: What three women are mentioned in the genealogy found in Matthew Chapter 1?

To kick off his gospel account, Matthew established a history of Jesus going all the way back to Father Abraham. (Genealogies were important to the gospel writers.)

Matthew's genealogy includes mostly names of fathers – but three famous mothers are mentioned as well. One of course is **Mary**, the mother of Jesus and wife to Joseph.

The other two women are **Rahab** and **Ruth**, the wives to Salmon and his son Boaz.

Salmon (son of Nahshon) married Rahab the harlot. Wow!

For background, read Joshua Chapters 2 & 6 about the story of Rahab. She was instrumental in allowing Joshua's spies to penetrate the walls of

Jericho, setting up its eventual fall. That was the beginning of the Israelite's entry into the Promised Land (Canaan).

Salmon and Rahab had a son, **Boaz**. Boaz married a lady named Ruth, the Moabite (not one of the 12 tribes).

Ruth was widowed and found herself in a similar predicament as the widow Tamar (remember, the mother of Perez).

So Ruth accompanied her mother-in-law, Naomi, back to Naomi's homeland (tribe of Judah). Ruth eventually remarried to Boaz. Since Ruth was not an Israelite, her role in the line of the Seed is stunning as well.

That's two straight generations of non-Israelite mothers!

And what's around the corner is quite special as well.

Ruth and Boaz had a son named **Obed**. And Obed had a son **Jesse**. And Jesse had a son named... David!

What a legacy!

If your children are old enough and have spent years in church, they likely know the stories of David and also the stories of Ruth. But did they know how these characters are related?

Take time to reinforce the big picture of this Advent Journey. The Bible is about a Seed that travels 4,000 years, covering 64 generations.

The Bible unfolds the family history of Jesus. We started in Eden with Adam, and we're working our way forward... to Bethlehem.

DAY 15

THE BIBLE'S MOUNT RUSHMORE

David (33)

[Scheduled Reading: 1 Chronicles 2:12-15]

Boaz fathered Obed, Obed fathered Jesse. ¹³*Jesse fathered Eliab his firstborn, Abinadab the second, Shimea the third,* ¹⁴*Nethanel the fourth, Raddai the fifth,* ¹⁵*Ozem the sixth,* **David** *the seventh.*

Who would you consider among the list of the most famous ancestors to Jesus Christ?

Adam? Noah? Abraham, Isaac and Jacob?

Make room for **King David**. His role was gigantic!

After the twelve tribes were led out of Egypt by Moses, they were led into the Promise Land by Joshua.

Over the next 300-400 years, the Israelites were led by a series of "judges."

Let's step back and look at the big picture.

The goal for these twelve tribes was to inhabit the land of Canaan. That's why God led Terah and Abram out of Ur, right? And Canaan is where Bethlehem is.

While settling in the Promised Land, they encountered various enemy groups. So God assigned military leaders – known as "judges" - to rally the twelve tribes and fight off these enemies.

For this era of "judges," think of MMA (mixed martial arts) fighters with swords, not pot-bellied men wearing robes.

Eventually the Israelites grew discontent with judges and requested a king.

God initially gave them King Saul (tribe of Benjamin) but later chose David as the replacement king.

One of the Bible's most famous seed-setting events is called the "Davidic covenant" – God promised David that his throne would last forever.

16 And your house and your kingdom shall be made sure forever before me. Your throne shall be established forever (2 Samuel 7:16).

Remember Jacob's blessing to Judah?

The scepter shall not depart from Judah, nor the ruler's staff from between his feet, until tribute comes to him (Genesis 49:10).

Judah's blessing was the first hint that kings would come from his seed. Sure enough, David was that king.

By the way, how does any kingdom last forever? History is filled with the rise and fall of one nation after another.

But God is talking about a divine kingdom – whose ruler will be Jesus Christ.

One thousand years after King David, Jesus would come to earth and be hailed as the King of the Jews. And one day still in the future, Jesus will resume his reign on earth and in the new heavens.

Jesus came from the line of kings, tracing its origins all the way back to King David.

If there was a Mount Rushmore for famous fathers of the Seed, it would have to include David!

> *Give the family a fun pop quiz.*
>
> *How many fathers in line of the Seed (up to King David) can you name together as a family (or separately, if you're a competitive bunch.)*
>
> *Remember — David is #33, so we're talking about those names we've covered so far in this Advent Journey.*
>
> *Have fun!*

DAY 16

THE BIG "IF"

Solomon (34)

[Scheduled Reading: 2 Samuel 12:24-25, 1 Chronicles 3:1-9]

*2 Samuel 12:24-25 - ²⁴ Then David comforted his wife, Bathsheba, and went in to her and lay with her, and she bore a son, and he called his name **Solomon**. And the Lord loved him²⁵ and sent a message by Nathan the prophet. So he called his name Jedidiah, because of the Lord.*

*1 Chronicles 3:1-9 - These are the sons of David who were born to him in Hebron: the firstborn, Amnon, by Ahinoam the Jezreelite; the second, Daniel, by Abigail the Carmelite,² the third, Absalom, whose mother was Maacah, the daughter of Talmai, king of Geshur; the fourth, Adonijah, whose mother was Haggith; ³ the fifth, Shephatiah, by Abital; the sixth, Ithream, by his wife Eglah; ⁴ six were born to him in Hebron, where he reigned for seven years and six months. And he reigned thirty-three years in Jerusalem. ⁵ These were born to him in Jerusalem: Shimea, Shobab, Nathan and **Solomon**, four by Bath-shua, the daughter of Ammiel; ⁶ then Ibhar, Elishama, Eliphelet, ⁷ Nogah, Nepheg, Japhia, ⁸ Elishama, Eliada, and Eliphelet, nine. ⁹ All these were David's sons, besides the sons of the concubines, and Tamar was their sister.*

David had several wives and nearly twenty sons. Which son did God choose to route the path of the Seed?

Answer: God elected an offspring of Bathsheba, the woman with whom David committed his infamous adultery.

The baby conceived out of adultery did not live. But after Bathsheba's husband died at battle (orchestrated by David), she became David's wife and together they conceived another child...Solomon .

God loved Solomon and showed great favor toward Him. God appeared to Solomon in a dream and promised him great wisdom, riches and honor.

Sure enough Solomon possessed honor and splendor beyond that of any king or person ever.

Solomon built a massive, elaborate temple. Solomon's temple was an impressive symbol of strength and prosperity for Israel...and most importantly, a symbol of God's favor and protection of the Israelite nation.

During Solomon's reign, God affirmed the Davidic promise to Solomon - that David's kingdom would endure forever.

But there was a big "IF" attached.

IF Solomon served and obeyed God, his kingdom would endure. But IF he turned from God, Israel would be torn from its land and the famous temple would be demolished.

Notice the big "IF's below"

*⁴And as for you, **if** you will walk before me, as David your father walked, with integrity of heart and uprightness, doing according to all that I have commanded you, and keeping my statutes and my rules, ⁵ then I will establish your royal throne over Israel forever, as I promised David your father, saying, 'You shall not lack a man on the throne of Israel.' ⁶ But **if** you turn aside from following me, you or your children, and do not keep my commandments and my statutes that I have set before you, but go and serve other gods and worship them, ⁷ then I will cut off Israel from the land that I have given them, and the house that I have consecrated for my name I will cast out of my sight, and Israel will become a proverb and a byword among all peoples. ⁸ And this house will become a heap of ruins. (1 Kings 9:4-8.)*

Tragically, Solomon failed the test. He chose the 2nd of the "Big IF's." Even in all his wisdom, his faith faded and he turned away from God and toward the gods of his foreign wives.

God initiated Israel's decline and removed His hand of favor and prosperity from Israel.

Of roughly forty known authors of the Bible, Solomon (credited for Proverbs, Ecclesiastes, Song of Solomon, and a few Psalms) was the only one to leave such a tainted legacy.

Israel's decline was one of the saddest reversals in Biblical history. And it was triggered by Solomon's walk-away from God.

It's hard to believe that the man credited for writing Proverbs, and other wisdom literature, made such poor choices and ultimately shipwrecked his faith (1 Kings 11:4-8).

How is this possible?

Discuss the relationship between knowledge and obedience. Wisdom and knowledge is essential, but ultimately obedience is what pleases God.

DAY 17

CHUTES AND LADDERS

Rehoboam (35)

[Scheduled Reading: 1 Kings 11:42-43]

*^{42} And the time that Solomon reigned in Jerusalem over all Israel was forty years. ^{43} And Solomon slept with his fathers and was buried in the city of David his father. And **Rehoboam** his son reigned in his place.*

If you're as old as me, you've likely heard of the Milton Bradley board game called *Chutes and Ladders*? (Kids still play the game today!)

A series of dutiful, steady-plodding upward moves toward the top of the board could be mostly undone by a single, massive slide – nearly all the way to the bottom.

This rise and fall describes the history of Israel.

Centuries of forward progress (for Israel) were reversed in a single generation.

From Abraham, to Isaac, to Jacob… and all the way to King Solomon – was fifteen generations of fathers in the line of the Seed. The era covered roughly one thousand years.

Aside from a few hiccups in the journey, everything seemed to be working for the Seed.

During this millennial season, the Seed departed from Ur and settled in Canaan (Abram), journeyed to Egypt to escape famine (Jacob), escaped from slavery back out of Egypt (led by Moses), entered the Promised Land (led by Joshua).

Along the way the Seed went from a small family, to a large family, to a collection of tribes, to a mighty nation.

As the Seed attained kingdom status, it achieved military dominance (David) and ultimately world-renowned wealth and prosperity (Solomon).

Next the Seed began a new trajectory - back to the bottom.

Just one man (King Solomon) triggered its downfall. God made the eventual downfall certain during Rehoboam's reign. **Rehoboam** was Solomon's son – and next in the line of the Seed.

Here's how the kingdom collapse unfolded (see 1 Kings 11).

1. God told Solomon his kingdom would be torn apart.

2. God would do so during Rehoboam's reign.

3. God affirmed His covenant with David (the forever kingdom) and promised to leave one tribe with Rehoboam.

Any idea which tribe would stay with Solomon and Rehoboam's seed? *Answer: Judah!*

God always has a plan to keep the Seed alive, right?

As God predicted to Solomon, the kingdom of Israel split into two kingdoms: the ten northern tribes (called "Israel" in Samaria) and two southern tribes (called "Judah" in Jerusalem).

[Note: the tribe of Benjamin stayed with Judah.]

So what's going on?

God is executing the terms of His promise: If you don't obey, you will suffer judgment.

To carry out the Seed strategy, God preserved the tribe of Judah. And Judah possessed Jerusalem… and yes, Bethlehem!

If you're a parent who remembers the game, Chutes and Ladders, draw a visual for the kids of the "Up-up-up-down all the way" slide action (stair-step up and dramatic slide down).

Talk about what it was really like for Israel to grow from a single family (Abraham) to a massive kingdom — only to be taken captive and exiled to a foreign land.

DAY 18

IN GOD'S SIGHT

Abijah (36), Asa (37), Jehoshaphat (38), Joram (39)

[Scheduled Reading: 1 Chronicles 3:10-11]

¹⁰ The son of Solomon was Rehoboam, **Abijah** *his son,* **Asa** *his son,* **Jehoshaphat** *his son,* ¹¹ **Joram** *his son,*

The next sixteen fathers in line of the Seed were kings. From the reign of Rehoboam when the kingdoms split, the kingdom of Judah lasted for just over three hundred fifty years (and roughly two hundred years for Israel).

These kingdoms were led by mostly evil kings, with occasional good kings.

Most of the time God dealt with kings and their respective kingdoms according to their behavior and countenance toward God.

They either "did right in the sight of the Lord" or "did evil…" He interceded for the righteous and inflicted judgment on the evil. Pretty straightforward.

To Rehoboam, God said "You have abandoned me, so I have abandoned you." Sure enough, Jerusalem was plundered by the Egyptians.

Occasionally God's judgment seemed delayed or absent. **Abijah** followed the pattern (evil) of his father Rehoboam, but he had success against his adversaries.

Next we have **Asa** and **Jehoshaphat** – both righteous kings. Both tore down the altars for idol worship and initiated worship reforms according to the law of Moses.

God honored both kings and gave them success against their enemies.

But when **Joram** succeeded the throne, he returned to the wicked ways of his great grandfather, Abijah. In fact, he killed his six brothers. (Yes, those were Jehoshaphat's sons!)

Despite this atrocity, the Lord was not willing to destroy the house of David because of His covenant with David (2 Chronicles 21:7).

God continued to have His way with the path of the Seed – seeking to fulfill His covenants and His overall promise from Genesis 3:15.

As we meet these kings along the Advent Journey, keep in mind – these men (even the most wicked ones) were ancestors to Jesus!

Bible Reading Tip!

When reading the Biblical account of kings, it helps to follow references to "Judah" and "Israel." Following the family lines, and bouncing back and forth between northern and southern kingdoms gets confusing.

First, there are lots of common names in both kingdoms (think of today's names like John, David, James, etc.) To add to confusion, intermarriage between Israel and Judah becomes tricky. But for students of Bible genealogies, it's fascinating how cleanly the Seed passes within the family for Judah. It's all because of God's promise to King David – that his seed would remain on the throne forever.

DAY 19

CLOSE CALL

Ahaziah (40), Joash (41), Amaziah (42), Azariah/Uzziah (43), Jotham (44)

[Scheduled Reading: 1 Chronicles 3:10-12]

¹⁰ The son of Solomon was Rehoboam, Abijah his son, Asa his son, Jehoshaphat his son, ¹¹ Joram his son, **Ahaziah his son, Joash his son,** *¹² Amaziah his son, Azariah his son, Jotham his son,*

It was a dismal decline for Judah.

Fending off outside enemies, fighting with Israel (northern kingdom), and there was always internal chaos - conspiracies, assassinations, take-over attempts. Business as usual for power-hungry, fear-driven monarchies.

Amazingly, the transfer of the Seed was never disrupted.

Unlike in the north (Israel) where kings bounced around from tribe to tribe, southern kingdom rule stayed within the tribe of Judah.

And while family succession for Israel occasionally hit a dead end - with no son to succeed the throne - Judah always seemed to find a way to pass the Seed. We're learning to expect that with God's Seed strategy, right?

There were some close calls, though.

For example, **Ahaziah** (son of Joram) reigned for a single year, before being assassinated by the king of Israel.

This assassination was ordained by God. (Just because Ahaziah was in the line of the Seed, did not guarantee God's protection.)

62

Then Ahaziah's mother, Athaliah, killed the remainder of the royal family - including Ahaziah's sons! (Yes, she murdered her grandbabies!)

But what about the Seed?

Thanks to God's sovereignty, Ahaziah's sister rescued Ahaziah's one-year old son, baby **Joash,** and stole him away. She hid the baby Joash in the temple for six years while Athaliah was ruling as Queen!

The Queen was eventually assassination by a priest (another God-orchestrated death). And Joash assumed the throne as a seven-year-old kid!

Unbelievable! That's called protecting the Seed!

Joash went on to be a good king – "doing what was right in the sight of the Lord." However, he turned toward evil in his later years.

Joash's son **Amaziah** followed a similar path. He started with a "good king" legacy. But he too turned away from God later in life.

(Notice the pattern of many kings – start good, finish bad.)

Next in line of the Seed was **Azariah (Uzziah)** and **Jotham.** Both were mostly good kings.

Meanwhile, something sad was about to happen up north for Israel.

After nineteen straight evil kings, Israel was invaded by Assyria. Its people were deported, bringing the end to the ten northern tribes.

They scattered and never returned to their identify as individual tribes or even as a kingdom.

Meanwhile Judah's captivity was coming soon, too. It was roughly one hundred fifty years away. They would also be exiled… but God had a plan for their eventual return.

And why did God plan a return for Judah and not for Israel?

Of course… the Seed.

How does a seven-year-old become a king? And how does a seven-year-old with such wicked ancestors (and no parents because they were killed) grow up to be a righteous king that seeks to follow God?

Discuss how Joash's aunt must have raised baby Joash to prepare him to be a king, and more importantly, to become a faithful child of God.

DAY 20

BAD KINGS, BAD SEEDS

Ahaz (45), Hezekiah (46), Manasseh (47), Amon (48), Josiah (49)

[Scheduled Reading: 1 Chronicles 3:10-14]

[10] The son of Solomon was Rehoboam, Abijah his son, Asa his son, Jehoshaphat his son, [11] Joram his son, Ahaziah his son, Joash his son, [12] Amaziah his son, Azariah his son, Jotham his son, [13] ***Ahaz his son, Hezekiah his son, Manasseh his son,*** [14] ***Amon his son, Josiah his son.***

For casual Bible readers reading through the Bible, the books of Kings and Chronicles feel like a completely different Bible.

The first half of the Seed journey contains a decorated faith legacy – men like Enoch-Methuselah-Lamech-Noah… and Abraham-Isaac-Jacob… and then men like Boaz and King David.

The line of the Seed has lots of bright spots. Men who were faithful. God-fearing. Spiritual giants.

Yes, they were sinners. They were human. But grace and forgiveness flowed in and out of the life accounts of these God-fearing men.

But as we enter the era of kings (after Solomon), it feels like a train wreck for the Seed. It's unfathomable how some of these characters ended up in the line of Jesus Christ!

Back to our Advent journey, the erratic see-sawing of good kings and bad kings continued for Judah.

After Azzariah and Jotham (both good kings), the next king, **Ahaz,** sinks Judah into deeper darkness. Among his many notables is having sacrificed his sons in the fire to the idol Molech!

Shockingly, somehow Ahaz's son, **Hezekiah**, grew up to be a great God-fearing king.

(Think about it, Hezekiah's very own brothers were sacrificed by their father Ahaz)!

Hezekiah sought to undo the sins of Ahaz and labored dutifully to restore worship reforms for Judah.

Then as the see-saw motion goes, Hezekiah was succeeded by a horrible King **Manasseh** (who also burned his son as an offering).

It's amazing that these children-sacrificing kings did not extinguish the Seed along the way!

After another evil king, **Amon**, Judah claimed another legendary God-fearing king, **Josiah.**

Josiah discovered the Books of the Law and once again restored the worship customs, feasts and sacrifices for Judah.

After a few more rotten kings, we're approaching the end of the line of kings. And Jerusalem is about to be captured and exiled to Babylon.

Did I just say Babylon? I thought this advent journey was headed away from Babylon...to Bethlehem?

What's going on?!

Sacrificing children in the fire was a dark evil that started with pagan nations. Now it's a problem in Israel and Judah!

If age appropriate, discuss with the children how this would have been a strategy of Satan to terminate the line of the Seed?

What are other biblical examples of rulers killing babies?

(Pharaoh of Egypt after Moses' birth, King Herod after Jesus' birth.)

DAY 21

BACK TO BABYLON

Jehoiakim (50) and Jechoniah (51)

[Scheduled Reading: 1 Chronicles 3:15-16]

10 The son of Solomon was Rehoboam, Abijah his son, Asa his son, Jehoshaphat his son, 11 Joram his son, Ahaziah his son, Joash his son, 12 Amaziah his son, Azariah his son, Jotham his son, 13 Ahaz his son, Hezekiah his son, Manasseh his son, 14 Amon his son, Josiah his son. __15__ ***The sons of Josiah: Johanan the firstborn, the second Jehoiakim, the third Zedekiah, the fourth Shallum. 16 The descendants of Jehoiakim: Jeconiah his son, Zedekiah his son;***

It never hurts to remind ourselves - the reason we're tracking the line of kings is because we're tracking the Seed!

With a few rare exceptions (i.e. Hezekiah, Josiah), the real Bible rock stars during this kingdom decline were not the kings. They were the prophets!

These prophets were not in the line of the Seed. Most were not even from the tribe of Judah (Daniel was an exception).

The prophets had what I call "dirty jobs." Their role was to tell the kings what God was planning to do.

The kings were mostly unreceptive and threatened to kill the prophets. Many prophets died gruesome deaths at the hands of wicked kings.

The prophet Isaiah told Hezekiah (good king) that a day was coming when all the kingdom treasures, and even the kings sons, would be carried off to Babylon. (2 Kings 20:16-19)

Yes, Babylon!

Sometimes God went to extremes to make a point. If God wanted to expose the people for their sins and humble them to their knees, I think exile to Babylon might do it.

Remember, God hated everything Babylon stood for. God led Abraham away from Ur (nearby Babylon) and toward an open spacious land so that the nation of Seed carriers could grow and thrive.

And now the Seed is going back to Babylon?! That's nearly fifteen hundred years backwards!

Sure enough, King Nebuchadnezzar of Babylon invaded Jerusalem and captured **King Jehoiakim.**

Later Nebuchadnezzar invaded again and this time carried off Jehoiakim's son, **King Jeconiah**, the royal family, all the royal treasures and the remainder of the inhabitants of Jerusalem (leaving behind only the poorest of the land).

Roughly ten years later (587 BC), Babylon returned and Jerusalem was finally, fully desolated and officially in exile.

There's supposed to be a special baby boy born in Bethlehem in about 590 years. But the Seed was stuck in Babylon!

Bible historians say the prophet Isaiah was martyred by being sawed in two by King Manasseh. Historians also say that Isaiah understood the mysteries of the coming Messiah (THE Seed) more than any other prophet.

Read Isaiah 7:14 as an example of one of Isaiah's great prophesies of the Seed.

DAY 22

THE SEED OF BABYLON

Shealtiel (52), Zerubbabel (53)

[Scheduled Reading: Haggai 1:14; 2:23]

*And the Lord stirred up the spirit of **Zerubbabel** the son of **Shealtiel**, governor of Judah, and the spirit of Joshua the son of Jehozadak, the high priest, and the spirit of all the remnant of the people. And they came and worked on the house of the Lord of hosts, their God, (Haggai 1:14).*

On that day, declares the Lord of hosts, I will take you, O Zerubbabel my servant, the son of Shealtiel, declares the Lord, and make you like a signet ring, for I have chosen you, declares the Lord of hosts." (Haggai 2:23)

———————————

Today we meet perhaps the most significant, <u>unfamiliar</u> name in the line of the Seed. His name was Zerubbabel.

And what does the name Zerubbabel mean? *Answer: "The Seed of Babylon."*

Zerubbabel was born in Babylon during Judah's exile! Wow!

Let's step back and look at a Big Picture prophecy.

According to the prophet Jeremiah (Chapter 25), God had some events planned:

1. Judah would be captured by Babylon and exiled from their land.

2. Babylonian captivity would last 70 years.

3. After 70 years, God will bring judgment on Babylon (conquered by Cyrus the Great of the Persian Empire).

4. A remnant of Judah would return to Jerusalem.

70

Those of us on the Advent Journey have the benefit of hindsight. These prophecies line up nicely with history.

But without this hindsight perspective, Babylonian exile was an unexpected detour for the Seed.

How would the Seed advance while the people were exiled in a foreign land? And not just any foreign land, but Babylon!

After Babylon was conquered, King Cyrus showed favor on the tribe of Judah and issued orders for Jerusalem to be rebuilt! (All part of God's amazing sovereignty – see Isaiah 44:28).

Zerubbabel found favor during Judah's exile and was positioned as governor of Judah. (Zerubbabel was grandson to the rotten King Jechoniah.)

Zerubbabel found himself at the center of yet another of the Seed's impressive pivot points. Zerubbabel hosted a return mission trip to Jerusalem to help rebuild the city (temple and walls).

The father-son combo, *"Zerubbabel, son of Shealtiel"* is referenced nearly a dozen times throughout the books of Ezra, Nehemiah and Haggai.

When we think of the Jerusalem rebuilding projects, we mostly think of Ezra and Nehemiah. Their names get the most press attention. But Zerubbabel's name is sprinkled all throughout.

Zerubbabel falls not only in line of the Seed – but also in a line of history's famous travelers who helped to transport the Seed during various pivot points.

The first was Abraham – transporting the Seed from Ur to Haran to Canaan.

Later God used Moses – directing the Seed out of slavery in Egypt.

Then roughly 1,000 years later, after an unexpected detour to Babylon, God used Zerubbabel – to get the Seed back to Jerusalem.

The Seed is going back home…near Bethlehem.

Years after king Jechoniah (Zerubbabel's grandfather) was exiled to Babylon, the king of Babylon released Jechoniah from prison and showed him unusual favor…affording him royal treatment, seating him among the kings and letting him eat from the kings table for the rest of his life.

What might explain this special favor given what we know about Zerubbabel's future assignment?

[Perhaps this favor extended to king Jechoniah was God's way of preparing the way for grandson Zerubbabel — so that he would be in position to return to Jerusalem as governor of Judah.]

DAY 23

SILENT NIGHTS

Abiud (54), Eliakim (55), Azor (56), Sadoc (57), Achim (58), Eliud (59), Eleazar (60), Matthan (61), Jacob (62)

[Scheduled Reading: Matthew 1:12-16]

*12 And after the deportation to Babylon: Jechoniah was the father of Shealtiel, and Shealtiel the father of Zerubbabel, 13 and Zerubbabel the father of **Abiud**, and Abiud the father of **Eliakim**, and Eliakim the father of **Azor**, 14 and Azor the father of **Zadok**, and Zadok the father of **Achim**, and Achim the father of **Eliud**, 15 and Eliud the father of **Eleazar**, and Eleazar the father of **Matthan**, and Matthan the father of **Jacob**, 16 and Jacob the father of Joseph the husband of Mary, of whom Jesus was born, who is called Christ.*

After the prophet Malachi, there were roughly 400 years of silent nights. Not the kind of peaceful evening we think of at the manger scene, where a mother cuddles her newborn Christ child.

I'm talking about the roughly 146,000 days of silence from God.

There are no biblical accounts to report between the last prophet Malachi and the Gospels (between the Old and New Testaments.)

No prophet stirrings. No angel appearances. Nothing.

But guess what? Bible genealogies do give us some nuggets from this era. The Seed carriers!

That shouldn't be surprising for us Advent Journey folks.

How special is it to know that the only mention of the 400-year silence is the fathers in line of the Seed!

Matthew's genealogy mentions nine fathers that carry the Seed forward from Zerubbabel. We know nothing else about these men.

The fact that we have their names says something about God's desire for us to have this precious Seed history.

If you read Luke's genealogical account (Chapter 3), you'll notice different names mentioned for this "silent" period.

That's because Luke reports the genealogy for Mary, while Matthew reports the genealogy for Joseph.

Mary is also from the tribe of Judah, child of King David – but her lineage traces to David's son, Nathan. Because Joseph is in the line of the kings (Solomon), the Bible is focused on that path.

Remember, Jesus comes from a line of kings.

Don't you imagine that for 400 years, some of the Jews were waiting for God to say or do something? Some were looking for the fulfillment of various prophecies and expected a king to arrive in the line of David.

What unfulfilled prophecies or promises are we still awaiting today? How might our waiting compare to that of the Jews during the 400 years of silence?

What encouragement can we gain from their example?

[Unfulfilled events – rapture of the church, 2nd return of Christ, future judgments, future reign of Christ, new heavens and earth.]

DAY 24

JOSEPH DID YOU KNOW?

Joseph (63)

[Scheduled Reading: Matthew 1:18-25]

*¹⁸ Now the birth of Jesus Christ took place in this way. When his mother Mary had been betrothed to **Joseph**, before they came together she was found to be with child from the Holy Spirit. ¹⁹ And her husband Joseph, being a just man and unwilling to put her to shame, resolved to divorce her quietly. ²⁰ But as he considered these things, behold, an angel of the Lord appeared to him in a dream, saying, "Joseph, son of David, do not fear to take Mary as your wife, for that which is conceived in her is from the Holy Spirit. ²¹ She will bear a son, and you shall call his name Jesus, for he will save his people from their sins." ²² All this took place to fulfill what the Lord had spoken by the prophet:*

²³ "Behold, the virgin shall conceive and bear a son, and they shall call his name Immanuel" (which means, God with us). ²⁴ When Joseph woke from sleep, he did as the angel of the Lord commanded him: he took his wife, ²⁵ but knew her not until she had given birth to a son. And he called his name Jesus.

If you're following this Advent Journey on schedule, today is Christmas Eve! The Bethlehem SEED is almost here!

Our journey brings us to Joseph, father to Jesus and husband to the Virgin Mary.

Joseph was engaged to a woman, Mary, whom he just learned was pregnant with child.

Very disturbing news.

Thanks to an angel encounter, and Joseph being a faithful man, he stayed the course and made it to the Bethlehem scene.

Naturally, Mary gets most of the attention in the Christmas story. A virgin teenage mother gives birth to the Christ child.

What a headline!

Often Joseph appears as a tag-along character, with shepherds, donkeys and goats. But as we've learned throughout this Advent Journey, Joseph's role and unique ancestry is monumental.

Joseph was from the line of the kings. Mary was not. Joseph's position in the line of the Seed was crucial to fulfilling the Davidic covenant – Jesus would come from a line of kings so that David's kingdom could endure forever.

I love the Christmas song, *Mary did you know?* But the Advent Journey has me thinking more about Joseph.

I wonder what he knew? How much did Joseph understand about his unique role in history?

Joseph did you know...

- That you came from a line of kings? (Matt 1:20, Luke 1:27).

- That you were a son of David? From the tribe of Judah?

- That your son would be "THE Seed" from Genesis (3:15)?

- That the prophet Isaiah was talking about your son when he wrote, "*Behold, the virgin shall conceive and bear a son, and shall call his name Immanuel*" (Is. 7:9)?

- That when you escaped to Egypt, with Mary and Jesus, to run from King Herod, you were protecting the Seed?

Joseph surely knew his lineage and where he came from. His angel encounter made some of this clear.

77

But I imagine it took time for him to fully process all that was happening and what it all meant — to be the earthly father to this Christ child.

Joseph's quiet, obedient nature is legendary… a fitting finish for this spectacular Seed journey.

I look forward to my own conversation with Joseph one day in heaven, to ask him questions about what he knew.

How do you see Joseph differently now that you understand his position in line of the Seed?

What questions might you have for Joseph, that you'd like to ask him someday in heaven?

DAY 25

B-O-O-M!

Jesus (64) [2ⁿᵈ Adam, Son of God]

[Scheduled Reading: Luke 2:1-7]

In those days a decree went out from Caesar Augustus that all the world should be registered. ²This was the first registration when Quirinius was governor of Syria. ³And all went to be registered, each to his own town. ⁴And Joseph also went up from Galilee, from the town of Nazareth, to Judea, to the city of David, which is called Bethlehem, because he was of the house and lineage of David, ⁵to be registered with Mary, his betrothed, who was with child. ⁶And while they were there, the time came for her to give birth. ⁷And she gave birth to her firstborn son and wrapped him in swaddling cloths and laid him in a manger, because there was no place for them in the inn.

For 25 days we've been following the Seed. Finally, on Christmas Day, THE Seed arrives in our Advent Journey.

We know the story. The manger scene. Mary and Joseph. Shepherds. Maybe donkeys and goats.

There's a star in the sky to mark this historic moment. But the real star of the story is down below, wrapped in cloth, sleeping comfortably on the hay as the song says. It's Baby Jesus.

Stepping back from the manger, let's look at the big picture.

It's a much larger story. We've been following it for 25 days. It's the story of two Adams.

We started in Eden – where the 1st Adam appeared, formed by God's hands from the dust of the ground.

Four thousand years and sixty-three generations later, the 2nd Adam appeared in Bethlehem as a newborn child, born of a virgin mother, conceived by the Holy Spirit.

Neither the 1st or 2nd Adam came from the seed of an earthly father. They were uniquely "sons of God" (Luke 1:35, 3:38).

The 2nd Adam came to redeem a fallen world – to atone for the sins started by the 1st Adam.

The Genesis 3:15 promise was one step closer to fulfillment. But the mission was not over yet.

The battle between good and evil was still raging. For four thousand years Satan sought to destroy the Seed. Even at the Bethlehem moment, the serpent was still at work.

A king named Herod issued a decree to kill all baby boys. He had heard rumors about this King of the Jews.

In a dream, an angel told Joseph to escape to Egypt with Mary and Jesus. THE Seed remained on the run from the enemy.

After Herod died, Jesus and his family returned to Nazareth where he grew up a Nazarene.

Then one day, after living a perfect life, he gave himself up as a living blood sacrifice, as a spotless lamb, for the sins of the world.

The 4,000 years of animal sacrifices were over. All the previous sacrifices were a picture of THE Seed on the cross.

A few days later, the unthinkable happened. Jesus returned to earth. THE Seed had been raised from the dead!

Still today the battle with the serpent is not fully over. Satan has much influence on earth. Sin is still alive.

One day in the future THE Seed from Heaven will return to take up His Church… those who have believed on Him for salvation of their souls.

And at some point later still, there will be another dark encounter with the enemy. There's an epic battle planned and a final fall of Babylon. (Yes, again! See Revelation 18.)

Then the "ancient serpent" will be captured and bound (Rev. 20:2).

After a period of time, the serpent will be released and then put away into a forever-burning lake of fire.

B-O-O-M!

Remember that sound from our Day 1 discussion? That's the sound of the Genesis 3:15 promise. When the seed of the women finally crushes the head of the serpent…forever.

What a plan! What a journey!

Merry Christmas, Friends!

You can read the Christmas story with your family at Matthew 1:18-2:23; Luke 2:1-21

It's been a privilege to share this Advent Journey with you. I hope it's been a blessing to you and your family, and I invite you to stay connected to future opportunities to engage with the Bible

Subscribe to my newsletter for more resources:

www.JeffAndersonAuthor.com

APPENDIX A

TRACKING "THE SEED"

1. Adam	22. Jacob	44. Jotham
2. Seth	23. Judah	45. Ahaz
3. Enos	24. Perez	46. Hezekiah
4. Cainan	25. Hezron	47. Manasseh
5. Mahalaleel	26. Ram	48. Amon
6. Jared	27. Amminadab	49. Josiah
7. Enoch	28. Nahshon	50. Jehoiakim
8. Methuselah	29. Salmon	51. Jechoniah
9. Lamech	30. Boaz	52. Salathiel *
10. Noah	31. Obed	53. Zerubbabel
11. Shem	32. Jesse	54. Abiud
12. Arphaxad	33. David	55. Eliakim
* Cainan	34. Solomon	56. Azor
13. Salah	35. Rehoboam	57. Sadoc
14. Eber	36. Abijah	58. Achim
15. Peleg	37. Asa	59. Eliud
16. Reu	38. Jehoshaphat	60. Eleazar
17. Serug	39. Joram	61. Matthan
18. Nahor	40. Ahaziah *	62. Jacob
19. Terah	41. Joash *	63. Joseph
20. Abraham	42. Amaziah *	64. Jesus
21. Isaac	43.Azzariah (Uzziah)	

* See Appendix B for Genealogy Notes

[Footnote: Genealogy from "A Family Tree: from Adam to Jesus" copyright © 2014, Genesis Japan https://usstore.creation.com/genealogy-poster]

APPENDIX B

BIBLE GENEALOGIES

There are several key genealogies throughout scriptures that help us piece together the lineage of Christ.

- ➤ Genesis 5 – first ten generations (Adam to Noah)

- ➤ Genesis 11 – next ten generations (Shem to Abraham)

- ➤ 1 Chronicles 1 & 2 - 33 generations (Adam to David)

- ➤ 1 Chronicles 3 - 20 additional generations (Solomon to Zerubbabel)

- ➤ Matthew 1 - partial ancestry of Joseph

- ➤ Luke 3 – ancestry of Mary

For the most part, these genealogies line up nicely. However, there are some discrepancies that require outside help. The main ones are presented below:

1. Luke's genealogy includes an additional name, "Cainan," between Shelah and Arphaxad (Luke 3:35-36). Neither Genesis 11 or 1 Chronicles include this name Cainan. There are various explanations, one which is a possible scribing error involved with the Hebrew to Greek translations.

    I included "Cainan" the list at Schedule A, but the name remains unnumbered in my Seed count.

2. Three successive kings – Ahaziah (40), Joash (41) and Amaziah (42) – are omitted from Matthew's genealogy, but are included in the Old Testament genealogy as well as the scriptures accounts of the kings (books of Kings and Chronicles).

    This is not a concern for most Bible historians as they note

84

Matthew's genealogical account is not intended to be complete. With a closer look, you'll notice Matthew presents three sets of 14 generations each, taking various liberties to accomplish his groupings. This makes sense if you compare a complete genealogy to Matthew's account.

3. Zerubbabel is identified as the "son of Shealtiel," over ten times throughout a variety of books – Ezra, Nehemiah, Haggai and in both Matthew and Luke's genealogical accounts. But the genealogy in 1 Chronicles (3:19) mentions Zerubbabel the son of "Pedaiah" (and Shealtiel as an uncle to Zerubbabel).

This discrepancy also doesn't seem to bother historians as they offer a variety of explanations, one being the common practice of a man taking custody of a brother's sons in the event of the brother's death. So if Pedaiah had died, Shealtiel would become father to the deceased brother's son (in this case, Zerubbabel.) We don't know this to be the case. This is just one of many possible explanations.

Bible genealogies are fascinating and fun to study as a family.

There's a cool genealogy poster available at Creation Ministries International (www.creation.com). This poster hangs on the wall in my home office. It reflects the 17th century work of James Ussher and mentions every father in the line from Adam to Christ, and well as some broader genealogical accounts of the other twelve tribes of Israel.

I highly recommend having this at home for further study and reference. https://usstore.creation.com/genealogy-poster

APPENDIX C

Timeline from Adam to Flood

Seed	Reference	Age when son born	Date
1. Adam	Gen 5:3	130	4004 BC
2. Seth	Gen 5:6	105	3874 BC
3. Enos	Gen 5:9	90	3769 BC
4. Cainan	Gen 5:12	70	3679 BC
5. Mahalaleel	Gen 5:15	65	3609 BC
6. Jared	Gen 5:18	162	3544 BC
7. Enoch	Gen 5:21	65	3382 BC
8. Methuselah	Gen 5:25	187	3317 BC
9. Lamech	Gen 5:28	182	3130 BC
10. Noah	Gen 5:32, 11:10	500	2948 BC
The Flood	Gen 7:6	100	2348 BC
Years from Adam to Flood		1,656 yrs	

Timeline from Flood to Abraham

Seed	Reference	Age when son born	Date
11. Shem	Gen 11:10	2*	2346 BC
12. Arphaxad	Gen 11:12	35	2311 BC
13. Salah	Gen 11:14	30	2281 BC
14. Eber	Gen 11:16	34	2247 BC
15. Peleg	Gen 11:18	30	2217 BC
16. Reu	Gen 11:20	32	2185 BC
17. Serug	Gen 11:22	30	2155 BC
18. Nahor	Gen 11:24	29	2126 BC
19. Terah	Gen 11:26	70	2056 BC
20. Abraham		0	
Yrs from Flood to Abraham		292 yrs	

* Shem had his son 2 years after the flood

ABOUT JEFF ANDERSON

Jeff Anderson speaks and writes about walking with God with an approach that combines scripture and story. He's the author of two books, *Plastic Donuts* and *Divine Applause* (Multnomah/Random House). Jeff and his wife, Stephanie, have four children.

WWW.JEFFANDERSONAUTHOR.COM

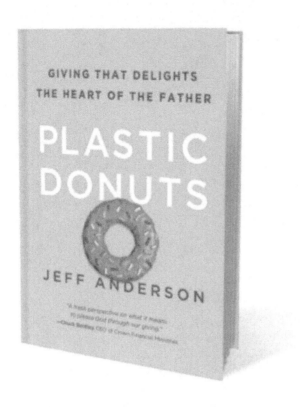

PLASTIC DONUTS IS THE STORY OF A SPECIAL GIFT THAT HELPED ME TO SEE GIVING FROM GOD'S PERSPECTIVE.

https://jeffandersonauthor.com/store/

Instead of bringing us closer to God, and each other, the topic of financial giving is murky for most believers.

This is why I wrote *Plastic Donuts*.

The message is the result of my deep-dive study of roughly 2,000 gift mentions in the Bible. *Plastic Donuts* takes away the awkwardness that so often accompanies the subject of giving, and replaces it with biblical clarity.

Contact us about free group-study resources, sermon notes, and campaign materials.

Jeff Anderson is a longtime friend. He is highly qualified to share the principles and practices of generosity with others because he personally lives them. Want to become more generous? Learn how from Acceptable Gift.

—Chuck Bentley, CEO, Crown Financial Ministries

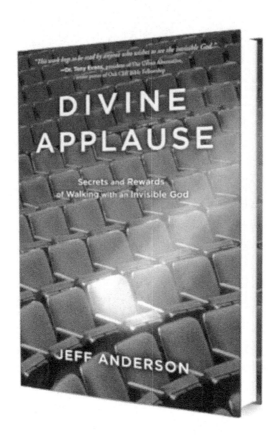

HOW DO WE HAVE A RELATIONSHIP WITH A
GOD WE CAN'T SEE?

https://jeffandersonauthor.com/store/

It's tough being separate from God, and even tougher because we don't know what we're missing. We can't hear His voice or see the Fatherly love in His eyes.

Or can we?

- Experience God's attention in unmistakable ways

- Cultivate an awareness of God's presence

- Enjoy the reward of secrets between you and God

- Take risks to break out of a status-quo life and connect more personally with God

- Discover how God is intensely interested in *you*

You don't have to settle for a silent or distant relationship with God.

God is invisible. At last we have a book that addresses this reality in a creative, refreshing, and encouraging manner.

—Dr. Richard Blackaby, author of *Unlimiting God,*
co-author, *Experiencing God*

This work begs to be read by anyone who wishes to see the invisible God.

—Dr. Tony Evans, President, The Urban Alternative.

Senior Pastor, Oak Cliff Bible Fellowship

POWER READ THE BIBLE

A COMPANION GUIDE FOR YOUR 60-DAY JOURNEY

You can read the entire Bible in 60 days. It's possible, surprisingly enjoyable, and faith expanding. This guidebook will help reframe your view of scripture. Jeff walks you though every step of the way with a proven reading plan, 60 days of encouragement, and eye-opening insights.

https://jeffandersonauthor.com/store/

Journey of the Seed
Catch the Bible's Big Picture in 60 Days

This reading challenge takes you from Genesis to Revelation with four important features:

- A focus on The Seed - the ancestry form Adam to Jesus
- A daily Bible reading plan yielding about one-third of the Bible
- Daily guidance and insights along the way
- Discussion points for you and your family

Made in the USA
Coppell, TX
14 November 2020